Inspiratic

CW00521181

To remind you of who you are when you forget

JACKIE WHIGHAM

INFINITE BEAUTY Publishers

Infinite Beauty Publishers
208 Waverly Crescent
Eliburn, Livingston EH54 8JT

Published by Infinite Beauty 2000

ISBN 0-9539626-0-1

Printed and bound in Great Britain by
Woolnough Bookbinding Ltd, Irthlingborough, Northamptonshire

Stay true to your Spirit
and you will succeed in everything you do

I have worked in the diet and fitness industry for over five years
and during this time the most common question asked is
"How can I stay motivated on my diet?"
To stay motivated you have to believe that you will succeed.
Unfortunately, the motivation we have in the beginning of our new
diet regime fades quite quickly because we expect overnight success.
When we don't get quick results we start to feed ourselves negative
information; it is here that we become demotivated.
We must remember that we are the creators of these attitudes.
It is the information we feed ourselves and the thoughts we hold onto
that set us up for failure and not the diet.

To stay motivated I recommend that you practise mind fitness exercises
on a daily basis. You must learn to create an environment in your mind
where self belief and success can be experienced. I suggest that you sit
quietly every day and silence your mind. Ask yourself what it is you
need encouragement with that day, then open the book at random.
Apply what you read into your life. Whenever you feel your motivation
starting to slide, continue to read the book until you feel your mind
return to a positive state.

This little book is here to remind you of who you are when you forget.

Introduction

*Over the past three decades, attention and emphasis
have been focused on food, weight and outer self. This
book has been written to shift the emphasis away from
these areas and towards a motivation springing from
within the individual ~ food for thought rather than food
for the body; a change from negative thinking into
positive thinking and to encourage and empower the
individual to believe that all things are possible. This
book is further intended to be a handy reference volume,
at any time, specially designed for the dieter between
classes or courses, giving them a continuing inspiration
and inner empowerment to carry on.*

INFINITE BEAUTY

Emotions

*There are only two emotions in the body –
one is love and the other is fear...*

Love

*...to function from a place of **love***
is to show compassion, understanding,
giving freely of yourself
with no returns,
laughter, peace...

Fear

*...to live from a place of **fear***
is to judge, criticise,
compare yourself with others,
compete, not seeing another's need
and to think that you are
different from others...

Your choice

*...which emotion
are you functioning from today?*

Be a best friend to yourself

*Would your best friend continue
to be your best friend if she undermined
you the way you undermined yourself?*

We're all equal

Stop comparing yourself with others.

Although we all look different on the outside,
we're all the same on the inside
and that's what counts.

This makes us all equal.

Stay with it

*No diet or fitness regime is going to
work for you
unless you work at it.*

Stay out of the problem

*Are you going to allow food to dominate
your thoughts today?*

*If you do, you're in the problem
and it's you who's putting you there.*

Focus on others' needs

Today take an interest in another person.

*The same interest that you would like
them to have in you.*

*This takes your mind away from
yourself and your problem.*

*Why do you think God made us
with two ears and one mouth?*

Be willing to learn

*If your middle name is "I know",
it means you are unteachable
and if you knew everything
then you wouldn't have a problem.*

Actions = Results

Knowledge without action = nothing.

Discipline your mind

*There is no point whatsoever
in having a slim, fit body
if you have
an unfit and undisciplined mind.*

Trust in the Process of Life

To know something is totally different
from experiencing it
and understanding it.

Know and trust that understanding will come.

Your Body

*Give up the fight you have
with your own beautiful body.*

No Excuses

The scales are not at fault,
you don't have a slow metabolism
or an under active thyroid gland

~ you're simply eating too much.

Be Honest with yourself

*You may have a thousand great new excuses
to overeat today
but I bet you don't have one good reason.*

You are Beautiful

*It wouldn't matter if the world agreed
that you were beautiful with a perfect figure*

*~ you wouldn't listen because
you don't believe in yourself.*

Shine Bright

*Your true beauty lies within you
and radiates from you out into the world,
not the other way around.*

Appreciate all of who you are

*If you don't change how you think
towards yourself now,
once you reach your goal weight
you will still continue
to find fault with yourself.*

*The only difference will be that
your body is smaller.*

*Why bother to lose weight
~ if you can't appreciate it?*

INFINITE BEAUTY

Open up your life

You can do absolutely anything
you want today
except
overeat or binge.

***Share** your happiness
with others*

*Practise being happy today,
most people are as happy as they decide to be.*

How to feel happy inside

Be positive in everything you say

~ to all whom you meet today.

You deserve the best

Always look your best,
regardless of your weight.

Live in this day

How do you stop struggling with your weight?

You accept where you are right here and now, but also be willing to make the necessary changes that will be required to make **your dream come true.**

Self Love

Be a good friend to yourself.

You have all power

Remember this ~
there is nothing wrong with you
which cannot be changed
without effort and discipline.

Keep your face to the Sun

*You're where you're meant to be right now,
so relax and keep moving forward.*

*You'll arrive at your goal weight
if you keep trying one day at a time.*

Courage - Go Forward

If you've had a bad eating day,
don't criticise yourself for not being perfect
~ stand up
~ dust yourself down
~ and start over again

...now...

don't wait until Monday.

Let go of the past

Remember what you ate yesterday is history.

You can't bring yesterday back.

*Treat each day as a new beginning
for growth and transformation.*

You can do it
- believe in yourself

If you think you're failing all the time,
do you just give up?

No, you keep trying new approaches
until you find the one that suits you.

Assert Your Power

Remember...
you're in control of your body
and not the other way around.

You deserve to succeed

*If you eliminate all your excuses
you can't help but succeed.*

Commitment

*Make a personal commitment to yourself
to be all you can be
~ and stand by it.*

What you give out
you get back

Remember that if you are only putting in
75% effort to your diet,
don't expect 100% results
at the scales.

The inner journey

Self-esteem comes from self and not from others.

Quietly keep repeating to yourself
~ over and over again ~
that you love and approve of yourself.

Courage

Don't be afraid of success.

It's your birthright.

Think about this!

*It's nice to be liked by others
and have their approval
but at the end of the day
it's only your opinion about you
that really matters.*

What is your opinion of you?

Today

*Start to appreciate
the beautiful person you really are.*

Take time to look

*It's nice for people to notice
how well you're looking
and how much weight you've lost
~ but it's even nicer ~*

if *you* notice.

Your strength is in your silence

*You don't have to tell people that you're on a diet
because what you do in private
shows in public.*

Think of others

If you're constantly hungry
it means you're constantly thinking about food
~ go and phone a friend
and take your mind away from yourself.

Self Honesty

*We're only afraid of the scales
when we're not doing
what we're supposed to be doing.*

Action is the keyword

Boredom lies in you,
not in your eating regime
or the world in which you live
~ go and do something new.

This will alleviate your boredom.

Befriend yourself

When you accept who you are
and where you are in life,
you stop fighting with yourself.

Action

*Do two things today that you don't want to
just for discipline; you'll feel great after it.*

Take responsibility
for your actions

Remind yourself today that it's no-one else's
fault for the weight you've gained.

Courage

Believe in yourself
~ you can do whatever you believe you can ~
just be willing to move out of
your comfort zone.

Think before you speak

Please don't judge
or criticise anyone today.

Careless words can only be offensive
and hurtful at another's expense.

Make today count

It's only what you do today that matters.

Become aware of your thoughts

If you don't like yourself
it's because of the negative information
you feed yourself.

The Power is within

The strength you are looking for
to stick to your diet
lies within you.

Believe in yourself.

Your feelings are part of who you are

*Don't suppress any more feelings with food.
Experience them and understand them.
They're not life-threatening.*

You deserve better

*To judge and criticise others
is to poison yourself.*

INFINITE BEAUTY

Being kind to yourself and others

Never be fooled.
True beauty is not reflected in the mirror,
it doesn't come from make-up
or nice clothes...
It comes from your heart and makes itself
known by how much you love yourself
...and others.

Sense of humour

Be flexible.
If you've had an extra two beans,
this doesn't mean that you've blown your diet.

Lighten up.

Inward journey

If you don't change from within,
then nothing in your outside world will.

Learning how to
Love Yourself

*Open up your mind and be willing to change
how you think and feel about yourself.*

*The easiest way to change is to say the opposite
of what you would normally say to yourself
every time you look in the mirror.*

Get rid of Excuses

How long have you been trying
to lose the same weight?

If it's more than two years,
you haven't made a decision to change it.

Why don't you
make that decision today?

Choose your words wisely

We teach people how to treat us
~ never criticise yourself in front of others,
not even as a joke.

Reflect

Do you have a self-destruction button?
What triggers it?

Clear Mind

*It's the obsession in the mind towards food
that destroys us more than the food itself.*

Destructive Thinking

*Today, don't talk or think about food or diet
and watch how difficult this is.*

*This exercise will highlight how obsessed
you are with your food problem.*

*It also highlights how much work
has to be done on your thoughts.*

Be a Winner

Stick with healthy, positive people.

Show the world you are happy

Smile at everyone you meet today
~ it's contagious ~
and what you give out comes back.

Change your thoughts

Food has no power over you
~ it only has the power you give it.

You give food power by
thinking about it all the time.

Strength

All the strength and power you need
to combat this problem
lies within you waiting for you to use it.

Happiness

*On this beautiful God-given day
what are you going to do
that will make you happy?*

Lighten up

Lighten up, have a good laugh.
Remember what it felt like to play
and have fun as a child.

The only time you ever thought about food
was when you were genuinely hungry.

Focus

*One of the laws of nature is
what you focus on you get more of,
so make sure you focus on what you want
rather than what you don't want.*

Focus on the final result.

Respect

If you can't look in the mirror
without criticising yourself,
then don't look until you can
respect and appreciate your body.

Work

*Remind yourself that
you don't just arrive at success,
you work towards it.*

Believe

Believe in yourself,
trust yourself
~ you can do this.

No excuses

Watch out for the excuses
you'll use tonight for a binge.

Self respect

Don't overeat today.

Give your body the respect it deserves.

Changing habits

If you keep saying "no, thank you"
it will become as easy as saying
"yes, please".

Self awareness

Every time you find yourself in the kitchen,
stop and ask yourself ~
"Am I hungry or bored?"

If bored, then make yourself busy.

Taking responsibility for yourself

*Who or what are you blaming
for your overeating?*

*Remember it's nothing to do with anyone else.
It's your problem.*

Positive attitude

Calories do count
but not as much as
a positive attitude.

Stand tall

Be aware of your posture.

Are you folded up
~ "poor me" ~
or are you straight and tall
~ "I'm in control" ?

Adjust your posture now and watch
how your attitude changes.

Don't use food to alter
how you feel

When you're overeating you're trying
to escape from some reality ~ acknowledge it
and work you're way through it.

It's the only way to stop destructive patterns.

INFINITE BEAUTY

Celebrate life

*Make this journey through life easier
by simply smiling.*

Focus on the solution

*When you're constantly thinking about food
you're focusing on the problem.*

*The solution is to take your mind
away from your obsession
and think of others or other things.*

Take time out to enjoy life

Today take time to look
at the beautiful surroundings
in which you live.

See how the trees salute you,
the flowers smile at you
and the grass calms you.

Breathe in the fresh air and be glad,
for these are God-given and free.

INFINITE BEAUTY

Strive to improve yourself daily

Change, change, change ~
how you look, how you speak
and how you act towards yourself and others.

This is how we improve ourselves
in the mind, body and spirit.

The power is within

There are no shortcuts to weight loss.

If there were,
you would have found them
by now.

Dance with life

*Spirituality is about having the spirit in you
to get up and live your life the way in which
it would make you happy
~ are you spiritually well today?*

Live today

Go and live your dreams.

You only have one life.

Don't throw it away on "if only".

Trust your own opinion

If you don't like others' opinions about you
~ then don't ask for them.

Self acceptance

Don't waste any more of your life
on not feeling good enough
because of your body shape or its weight.

You're much, much more than this.

Stop waisting time

How many years
have you wasted already
complaining about the same problem?

The past has gone

Are you still living in past glories?
They go something like this ~
"I used to be 'x' amount of pounds".
It's always "I used to be".

All that's really important is
what and where you are today,
because that's all you've got.

Inner freedom

Let go of everything that is holding you back from being who you want to be.

Be kind with your words

Don't judge or criticise others
because we're all going the same way.

Always extend the
hand of friendship

If you put your hand out to help others,
others will put their hand out to help you.

If you stick your foot out to trip others,
you'll find that others will do this to you.

It's the law of nature,
what you give out will come back multiplied.

INFINITE BEAUTY

*Gratitude is the
gateway to happiness*

*Just be grateful for another day of life
and count your blessings.*

Know and trust you will get there one day at a time

Keep going ~ you'll get there one day.
It will start with the loss of your first pound
which will then go to half a stone
~ then your first stone.

It's the same procedure for everyone,
so why should you be any different?

No-one gets overnight success.

Action

Keep your mind and body busy ~
preferably out of the kitchen.

Stop procrastinating

*There is no right time to start a diet,
only NOW.*

Zest for life

*Enthusiasm is a quality
you cultivate from within.
It's not something that will come
knocking on your front door.*

You deserve the best and no less

You only get in life
what you believe you deserve.

Keep your vision

*Morning, noon and night keep visualising
what you want to look like at goal weight.*

*Once you believe in this mental picture,
it will automatically be your reality.*

Your attitude is your choice

How is your attitude today?

*Is it positive and constructive
or negative and destructive?*

Either way it's your choice.

Your thoughts create your feelings

You can choose at any given moment
to be happy,
no matter what's going on in your life.

Stop hurting yourself

Don't you think it's sad
that a holiday snap is the shock treatment
we need to take ourselves in hand?

Keep looking within

*There is nothing outside of you
which has the power to make you overeat
if you don't want to.*

Change now

If you don't
deal with a problem today
~ you'll be sitting this time next year
with the same problem.

Be grateful for what's in your life now

Most people don't know what they have
or how well they are doing until they lose it.
Don't let this happen to you.

Acknowledge how well you are doing.

Limitations only exist in your mind

*If you are overweight and unfit it's you who did this to yourself ~ therefore it's **only you** who can change it.*

Compassion and understanding towards others

*You know the nice thing
about having a weight problem is this
~ you would never criticise anyone else
with a weight problem ~ why?*

Because you understand.

To change you must firstly become aware

Your thoughts create feelings and actions ~ therefore if you don't like how you're feeling or behaving, change your thoughts.

You are unique - you always will be

Feeling ashamed and embarrassed about your body will only keep you eating.

Learn to appreciate and love your body for where it's got you until now.

Sharing

If you can't lose weight for yourself
in the beginning,
then do it for someone
who cares deeply for you...

until you can do it for yourself.

You are not above or beneath anyone

*If you keep saying "It's all right for her",
it's this* **attitude** *which keeps you stuck and
not the person you're comparing yourself with.*

Put on your dancing shoes

The world doesn't owe you a living.

You owe it to yourself because you're alive.

Know what you want

To make a decision and commitment
to yourself is the foundation
upon which you will build your diet.
This foundation ~
(your mind)
has to be strong and precise.

The beginning is now

You can start your day at any time,
you don't have to wait another 24 hours.

A light mind will create a light body

You will automatically become lighter when you let go of all the pressures you put on yourself with diets, food, weight and body size

~ release all of these heavy thoughts ~

and let them go.

INFINITE BEAUTY

Cultivate gratitude

*Rather than looking at how much weight
you can lose because you've exercised
three times this week ~
try looking at it
from a point of view of gratitude.*

*Be grateful that you had
the health and money to do it
because some people don't have these luxuries.*

Everyone is your teacher

You only see in others
what's lying dormant in you,
or how else would you see it or understand it?

Your words define who you are

Your words are very powerful.

*Make sure you only speak
words of encouragement and understanding
to yourself and others.*

Polish the window of your mind

If you feel the world's out to get you
~ take a look inside ~
and see where you're attacking the world.

INFINITE BEAUTY

Do

To get results,
***Action** is the keyword.*

Positive self talk

*It's you who has to walk around with you
all the time with no breaks –
make sure you're on the best of talking terms
with yourself.*

Look beyond

Next time you're about to overeat,
fast forward the picture
and see the effects of this action.

Now do you still want to overeat?

Redirect your mind

If your mind becomes undisciplined
and strays to thoughts of ~
*"One **small** cake won't do me any harm"*
or
"I'll be really good tomorrow" ~

Tell yourself NO, NO, NO ~
don't go against the commitment you made to yourself.

Inner cleansing

*Clean up the inside of your body
with correct thinking and action
and the outside will take care of itself.*

Honour, truth and integrity

If you don't feel comfortable in life,
you're either doing something you shouldn't
or you're not doing something you should.

No limits

Never underestimate your abilities.

Break the chains

It's only you
who can free your mind and body
from this obsession towards food.

Fulfilment

Today love, live and laugh.

Courage to go forward

*You can't get the body you want
until you have the **courage**
to give up the old one.*

To give is to receive

*The helping of others nourishes your own spirit –
because you are giving of yourself.*

Nature heals

Peace will heal you.

Go and take a walk in a beautiful country park.

You are a light in this world

The closer you stick to nature
the closer you will get to your own essence
which is *love*.

Radiate happiness

Should you enter into a dark room today,
shine bright,
light it up
and be an example to others.

Give freely

*Tolerance, patience,
understanding, compassion,
joy and laughter = LOVE.*

Lay the foundations

*What can you do today to build you
a better tomorrow?*

Make peace of mind a priority

The only way to have peace of mind
is to give up the thoughts
which are causing you distress.

It's your choice
whether you want to keep them
or let them go.

Travel lightly

*Fear of the future is extra baggage
you can do without.*

*To live in the past will rob you of your future,
therefore live in the day.*

There's a gift for you from everyone

Take time to think of all the people who love you and who have added to your life...
and be thankful.

Make your mirror reflect beauty

*Always remember that you judge the world
by the inside of yourself.*

*What you see out there is only a mirror
of what's going on inside you.*

Keep showing love

When you have no enemies in your mind
you think everyone loves you.

You are a miracle

One of the finest acts of self love
is just to be yourself.

You're good enough,
kind enough,
loveable enough,
generous enough
and much, much more.

You always were.

Be an angel

*Be a good example to others
with the way in which you speak,
act and dress.*

*Only take in the good
and leave the rest*

*See good things,
look at good things,
read good things
and watch good things.*

*Feed your mind
with positive and nourishing thoughts.*

Use your wisdom

Only listen to good words
and cancel the rest out.

Self awareness

If I were to ask you the question ~
"Why haven't you lost the weight you've gained ?"

Write all the reasons (excuses) down on paper
and you will see clearly the thoughts and beliefs
which are still holding you back.

Break free from bad habits

Don't get frustrated with your weight.

You're not trapped.

*You can change anything about yourself
at any time you choose.*

Letting go

Having regrets
about the past is a waste of energy.

Once you accept the past and let it go,
peace will return.

Meditation

Take time today to sit and be still.

*Listen to your breath and empty your mind
of all the thoughts which are holding you back
from being who you want to be in this world.*

*As you listen to your breath
it will help you to get in touch with
your inner peace.*

Enlightenment is the gateway to truth

To be enlightened is to know who you are.

When you know who you are you understand that we are all the same...LOVE

Inner beauty

*Do you see a person's beautiful smile first
or that she has gained/lost too much weight?*

Where is your focus?

*Look towards the inside
rather than the outside.*

Make someone happy

To compliment someone is
music to your soul,
and music to the recipient's ears.

Everything in life is only on loan

Let thoughts, people, places and things
float in and out of your life freely,
you don't own any of them.

It's our attachment to them
which causes us stress.

Love yourself and others

*Your true beauty lies within you
and radiates from you out into the world,
not the other way around.*

If you wish to receive any further information on:-

Seminars
Workshops
Classes
Books

please write to:-

Jackie Whigham
208 Waverly Crescent
Eliburn
Livingston EH54 8JT